WE CAN ALL GET ALONG

IF...

Compiled by
Students of the Tales
cultural journalism project

A*t the time the idea for Project Get* *Along first came up, I thought it was interesting and had possibilities but was somewhat limited in scope. How many ways, I wondered, can you respond to,* *"We can all get along if ..."?*

But when the young people I was working with seemed taken with the idea, I thought it worthwhile because it would make people think about how we can all get along. Out of the death, destruction and division resulting from the verdict of the four Los Angeles policemen in the Rodney King incident, his question is still worth thinking about long after the emotion of the moment has subsided.

In a rapidly changing world, many people cling to their racial and cultural identities and refuse to tolerate and accept differences in others. With the downfall of communism in Eastern Europe and the Soviet Union, democracy seemed to be the answer to people who had known oppression for years.

Given the choice of democracy, however, many people began oppressing people unlike themselves, ethnic outsiders or recent immigrants fleeing oppressive governments. Of course, people all over the world have these racial and cultural biases and oppress people.

In this unstable climate, the project was born. It was spread by mail, electronic mail, personal contact and the media. Students in the project were interviewed by newspaper, radio and TV reporters about what they were doing and why. Responses started arriving.

Even from the early responses, it became apparent that the possibilities weren't so limited. Each response reflected a unique individual who cared enough about the question to give it some thought and share it with us.

And while we were learning about the unique perspective of others, the people connected with the project learned a bit about themselves and the world around them. Sometimes responses came as complete surprises.

One request was sent out over Internet, an electronic mail network reaching around the world, asking for responses from all over the country. We got them. But we also got a response from an angry young man in Sydney, Australia.

"We could all get along," he wrote, "if you bloody Americans would quit thinking that you're the only people with Internet access. Think before you post."

We've thought a great deal since then. And we've selected many different and interesting responses from around the country, and a few from around the world, too. The answers won't change the world, I'm sure. But there's a lot of common sense from a wide range of people that is worth taking a few minutes to consider and think about from time to time.

Ray Elliott
English & Journalism Teacher
Urbana High School, Urbana, Illinois
& Editor of Tales

A Letter Received By Project Get Along

People *have questioned using Rodney King's plea, "Can we all get along?," as the impetus for Project Get Along. Questioning that merit symbolizes what is wrong with this country. We are too quick to judge, condemn, categorize, criticize and put down people instead of offering a hand and accepting, understanding and trying to help people.*

I believe it all goes back to how we were treated as children. Those of us who have been involved in drugs, drinking too much, violence, breaking the law, eating too much, arrogant behavior and stepping on other people, among many other abusive, compulsive behaviors, have something in common: In one way or another, we were mistreated as children. The statistics related to child abuse are unbelievable. Too many of us were physically and/or sexually abused.

But many more of us suffered a more subtle form of emotional or psychological abuse. The abuser often didn't even know what he/she was doing. In trying to help us, they criticized us, told us what was wrong or bad about us instead of what was good and paid careful attention to our negative behavior while they ignored any positive behaviors. But they didn't help us. They made us feel insecure, self-destructive and bad about ourselves. We lashed out at others, as well as ourselves. We carried on the cycle. We looked for love in all the wrong places. We looked for comfort in drugs, alcohol, food, gangs, the crowd from the wrong side of town.

Instead of criticizing and judging Rodney King, let's congratulate *him for trying to make a bad situation better by asking, "Can we all get along?" Let's start looking for the good in people, regardless of how hard we have to look. Let's focus on the positive. Let's try to understand and look past the negative.*

Anonymous

"Can we all get along?"

Rodney King
at a press conference
May 1, 1992

WE CAN ALL GET ALONG IF ...

... we find that the things that seem to separate us can actually bring us closer together.

— 21, Marietta, OH

... everybody takes responsibility for his or her life and understands that individual freedom only goes to the point that it infringes upon the rights of others.

— 52, Urbana, IL

... you can give more and try a little bit harder.

— 17, Taipei, Taiwan

WE CAN ALL GET ALONG IF ...

... we get both sides of the story.

— 18, Sacramento, CA

... you try to think before you speak or act and don't be grouchy.

— 10 3/4, Urbana, IL

... all weapons were made into Gummy Bears.

— 16, Rostock, Germany

... people would take the time to learn about those who are different from them. Education is the key to getting along.

— 32, Newark, NJ

WE CAN ALL GET ALONG IF ...

... more people took the advice my parents always said, "If you can't say anything nice, don't say anything at all."

— 15, Urbana, IL

... we try.

— 20, Lake Placid, NY

... we try to understand each other and if we treat other people the way we would like to be treated ourselves.

— 16, Moscow, Russia

WE CAN ALL GET ALONG IF ...

... everybody understood the things people go through.

— Washington Park, IL

... we share and think twice before doing stupid things.

— 14, Nairobi, Kenya

... we never got older than 5 years old, but could take care of ourselves, and never had to worry about anything but who was bringing the cookies and milk.

— 17, Urbana, IL

WE CAN ALL GET ALONG IF ...

... we learn to communicate effectively. If we begin teaching our children how to speak clearly and listen with respect, we can change the direction of the world.

— 21, Phoenix, AZ

... we held ourselves accountable for our own actions. When we stop blaming our environment and childhood for our shortcomings, we will not have excuses to hide under to save our own pride. Then truth and honesty will be the foundation on which we build our house of respect for one another.

— 18, Hialeah, FL

WE CAN ALL GET ALONG IF ...

... we open ourselves up to learn from each other.

— 23, Middletown, OH

... there was enough food for everybody and if we had homes for everybody.

— 14, Urbana, IL

... we love each other.

— 14

... we give each other an equal chance. A person is a person, no matter how we were created.

— 18, Washington, IN

WE CAN ALL GET ALONG IF ...

... people learn that colors or cultures aren't bad but unique. They should learn that being different is something you should appreciate.

— 15, Urbana, IL

... everyone would just respect people no matter what ethnic background they came from. Try to make friends with someone different from you. It might help.

— 14, Edmonds, WA

... you put yourself in someone else's shoes before you begin to judge.

— 16, San Antonio, TX

WE CAN ALL GET ALONG IF ...

... we see ourselves and all others as valued and valuable contributors to the survival of our world.

— 35

... every living human being on this planet would have equal rights to be free, to live and think as they please, so long as they don't break the laws of their country.

— 60+, Cape Coral, FL

... everyone was not only willing to take but give.

— 14, Urbana, IL

... people in the United States will stop imposing their values and morals on the rest of the world.

— Hume, IL

... we break the cycle and stop reliving the past, we believe individuals can make a difference, we realize we are all "you people," we remember what we learned as children—share, treat others the way you want to be treated, take turns, listen and don't hit girls, we offer a helping hand instead of criticism, and we stop blaming each other.

— 34, Hickory Hills, IL

... we work together as a brother and sister in Jesus Christ.

— 31, Miami, FL

WE CAN ALL GET ALONG IF ...

... we don't worry about little things like race and concentrate on the bigger things.

— 14, Georgia

... we stop harping on the mistakes of the past and concentrate on the goals of the future.

— 18, Urbana, IL

... we would not celebrate our differences as much as embrace our similarities.

— 50, Raleigh, NC

WE CAN ALL GET ALONG IF ...

... we would be less superficial so we could spend more time educating and bettering ourselves.

— 18, Urbana, IL

... we don't criticize, condemn or complain and remember that a person's name is, to that person, the sweetest and most important sound in any language.

— 45, Cape Coral, FL

... we pray for peace and make the change in ourselves first. We must look at one another as equals, brothers, sisters, family, and learn to help and live together on this planet we call Earth.

— 18, San Antonio, TX

WE CAN ALL GET ALONG IF ...

... we trust each other and say nice things about each other and help each other with problems.

— 11, Urbana, IL

... people don't let their pride get in the way.

— 20, West Chester, OH

... we share a toy.

— 4

... people give a little more and try a little harder.

— 13, Eugene, OR

WE CAN ALL GET ALONG IF ...

... we all drink water from the same well.

— 16, Jakarta, Indonesia

... we all lived like the Smurfs. They have money, but they all work out of the goodness of their hearts, and they help each other when needed.

— 14, Urbana, IL

... we have opened minds and give each other a chance.

— 16, Los Angeles, CA

... we stick together and help one another and if we can come together for each other.

— O'Fallon, IL

WE CAN ALL GET ALONG IF ...

... we made snow angels together in the winter and picked daisies
together in the summer.

— 17, Urbana, IL

... we wouldn't laugh at people or call people names.

— 10, Richmond, VA

... everyone realized that we are all equal in the eyes of God. He made us
all with the same physiology. Blood runs through our veins; bones and
skin form every human being on this Earth. Therefore, there must be a
similarity among us all.

— 16, Sao Paulo, Brazil

WE CAN ALL GET ALONG IF ...

... all the money in the world is destroyed.

— 14, Jakarta, Indonesia

... we could accept differences without being frightened of them, understand differences without trying to force changes, seek the good in other people and not search for what is wrong with those who are different, and be fair with people of all colors in lieu of giving preferential treatment to those who are like us.

— 46, Urbana, IL

... we stop making fun of everybody and make friends.

— 10, Boys Ranch, NM

WE CAN ALL GET ALONG IF ...

... we really want to and then try working at it, treating one another with respect and helping them in a way that we would want to be treated and helped, building one another up in the ways of the Lord and loving with a pure love.

— 74, Lawrenceville, IL

... everyone had the same education.

— 15, Victoria, Hong Kong

... there weren't any stuck-ups or snots.

— 16, Urbana, IL

WE CAN ALL GET ALONG IF ...

... we share things that we have. Some people don't have the things others have. People like to share with other people sometimes. That's how we get along with each other.

— 15, Brady, TX

... we try to be the best role model for our children.

— 42, Urbana, IL

... we form a conference of all cultures and decide peace.

— 13, Edmonds, WA

... we help people pick up their Crayons and pencil
— 5, Richmond, V

WE CAN ALL GET ALONG IF ...

... we try, we share our lives, we communicate with each other, we work together toward the same goal, we make our children believe and we have a reason.

— 33, Valparaiso, IN

... we have God's love in our hearts and live according to what His love tells us.

— 16, Miami, FL

... we recognize, accept and respect differences that are inherent to each other's ethnic and cultural backgrounds.

— 17, Urbana, IL

WE CAN ALL GET ALONG IF ...

... we forget about looking good and tell the truth.

— 47, Boulder, CO

...people would stop believing everything they see on TV and remember that there is always more to the story than the media tell us.

— 44, Eagan, MN

... we stop labeling each other.

— 17, Urbana, IL

... we cause random acts of senseless kindness.

— 14, Blantyre, Malawi

WE CAN ALL GET ALONG IF ...

... we stop thinking people are stupid or weird because they are different.
We shouldn't start a fight or riot just because we don't like someone.

— 10, Urbana, IL

... we could see through the eyes of a child when we look at another
human being. As children, we knew not of prejudices which are instilled
in us as we become adults.

— 41, Cape Coral, FL

... we are aware and sensitive to other people's needs.

— 24, Evansville, IN

WE CAN ALL GET ALONG IF ...

... we try and forget about the past and start anew. The children of today do not know racism; they are taught racism.

— 21, Chicago, IL

... we get rid of all the bad people in the world.

— 13, Eugene, OR

... remember that the whole is only the sum of its parts. People need to wrestle with their ignorance, prejudice and fear and realize that until we are all free—no one can be free.

— 22, Urbana, IL

WE CAN ALL GET ALONG IF ...

... everyone ran naked in a warm summer rain.

— 16, Urbana, IL

... we would learn to talk through our problems.

— 10, Richmond, VA

... we can appreciate our differences and see value in diversity of the people of America, realizing that everyone has worth and a place in our multicultural society. Our people are like pieces of a multicolored quilt: together we are beautiful, strong and able to give the world comfort.

— 43, New Carlisle, IN

WE CAN ALL GET ALONG IF ...

... we act more mature. Then this world wouldn't be such a mess.

— 10, Urbana, IL

... we would just help each other out in desperate times and take pride in what we do.

— 55, Miami, FL

... everyone would go out to the forest and have a picnic.

— 17, Taipei, Taiwan

... we could realize that the color of your skin doesn't matter.

— 13, Eugene, OR

WE CAN ALL GET ALONG IF ...

... parents stop teaching kids racism. If kids of all ethnics are put in a playpen, they would play—until someone says it's wrong.

— 14, Edmonds, WA

... we respect one another, we love one another, listen to each other, feel each other's pain and support one another.

— 37, Valparaiso, IN

... teenagers had cheaper insurance rates.

— 16, Urbana, IL

WE CAN ALL GET ALONG IF ...

... we can be respectful to our neighbors and the people that surround us in our community.

— 56, Miami, FL

... we use love as global currency.

— 16, Jakarta, Indonesia

... we were color blind.

— 15, Urbana, IL

... you give love. Then you will receive love. If you give hate, you will receive hate.

— 23, Hialeah, FL

WE CAN ALL GET ALONG IF ...

... Elvis were still alive.

— 13, Champaign, IL

... people kept their opinions to themselves and if people stopped trying to be like the people in some movies.

— 14, Brady, TX

... as parents, spouses, neighbors, co-workers, we take time for each other—whether it be taking a child to the library or helping fix a car. Slow down and share some of your time.

— 42, Urbana, IL

WE CAN ALL GET ALONG IF ...

... we conquer our fears.

— 21, Milwaukee, WI

... people wouldn't get mad about piddly things or get in fights about useless things that don't mean anything.

— 11, Urbana, IL

... we be nice.

— 5, Coeymans, NY

... we start sending our kids to school instead of jail.

— 33, Hickory Hills, IL

WE CAN ALL GET ALONG IF ...

... we forget our delusions of a perfect world with perfect people and accept people and this world for what they are and work with reality and not demand fantasy.

— 24, Champaign, IL

... we all listen to the wiseness of our grandparents.

— 14, Nairobi, Kenya

... the white man stops treating us blacks like s---.

— 16, Urbana, IL

WE CAN ALL GET ALONG IF ...

... we judge people because of their character, not the color of their body.

— 13, Edmonds, WA

... we cheer up.

— 17, Urbana, IL

... we educate ourselves in the cultures of our peers, celebrating diversity instead of moving to destroy it and remembering that most of us are immigrants. Had our ancestors had to deal with the kind of intolerance that grips the country today, many of us would never have been born American—or even been born at all.

— 22, Baltimore, MD

WE CAN ALL GET ALONG IF ...

... each of us takes responsibility for our own lives and actions, if each of us remembers that other people's lives and actions are their responsibility and if each of us remembers that we are all members of the same species.

— 29, Naperville, IL

... people would swallow their pride and say they're wrong.

— 10, Richmond, VA

... we don't force anyone to do anything they don't want to do.

— 11, Urbana, IL

WE CAN ALL GET ALONG IF ...

... everyone would realize that life is short and too important to spend arguing over issues that should have been put to rest a long time ago. Working together is the only solution.

— 24, Miami, FL

... we don't have competitions on who is No. 1.

— 17, Taipei, Taiwan

... everybody would give warm fuzzies and smile.

— 17, Urbana, IL

WE CAN ALL GET ALONG IF ...

... we learn how to feel compassion for one another. Feeling compassion requires that we know about the challenges and joys of lives lived differently than our own. Without compassion, anger and resentment are rife because we see only the impact of others' behaviors on our own lives, rather than also seeing the circumstances and pressures shaping their lives.

— 42, Madison, WI

... all were to join as one.

— 18, Urbana, IL

... we can smile the same way we did as babies.

— 16, Jakarta, Indonesia

WE CAN ALL GET ALONG IF ...

... every race just acts like we're the same color, just acts like one huge family. Everybody is kin to each other, and everybody should be helping each other.

— 13, Brady, TX

... we share our feelings without fighting and cursing, find out different ways to help out people who need help, make organizations to support the homeless and the needy, and stop all violence and crime.

— 13, Champaign, IL

... we understand each other.

— 18, Ch'ongju, South Korea

WE CAN ALL GET ALONG IF ...

... if we sow faith and hope where there is doubt and despair.

— Unknown

... we work to continually educate ourselves and those around us about diversity and the wonderful differences between people. If we learn about each other, we can respect each other. If we can respect each other, our chances are better for understanding and getting along.

— 21, Madison, WI

... we just would not call people names and say nice things instead.

— 13, Urbana, IL

... we don't fight, don't punch or h
and solve our problems rig
— 4, Richmond, V

WE CAN ALL GET ALONG IF ...

...we had nothing except each other.

— 13, Eugene, OR

... we look for some way to help someone else each day.

— 39

... we realize the only way of life is peace. If we don't start getting things together soon, we might have a war among ourselves.

— Unknown

... people watch less T.V.

— 16, Urbana, IL

WE CAN ALL GET ALONG IF ...

... we all just would follow Martin Luther King's dream.

— 13, Edmonds, WA

... we do stuff together like picking up stuff on the ground and doing what our moms and dads tell us to do.

— 12, Urbana, IL

... we take the time and effort to understand others' motivation and point of view.

— 45, Cape Coral, FL

WE CAN ALL GET ALONG IF ...

... everyone had a good attitude and helped one another. Maybe if everyone would help one another, this world would be a better and safer place to live.

— 14, Brady, TX

... we could get rid of all the politicians in the world.

— 13, Champaign, IL

... we learn to place emphasis on others' needs, rather than on our wants.

— 25, Apple Valley, CA

WE CAN ALL GET ALONG IF ...

... we aren't afraid of our peers because of the way they look or act.

— 16, Urbana, IL

... we would have respect for others, be good listeners to understand what we are really saying and try to live by the Golden Rule.

— 72, Cape Coral, FL

... everyone disagreed with opinions instead of people.

— 15, Champaign, IL

... we all cooperated.

— 14, Bartonville, IL

WE CAN ALL GET ALONG IF ...

... we don't talk about someone behind their back, don't hit people for no reason, and don't tell someone something and tell another person something else.

— 13, Champaign, IL

... we can communicate with each other without any obstacles and learn to love one another as we are.

— 34, Miami, FL

... people look past color, race and income and look at who a person really is and what they have to offer.

— 16, Calumet City, IL

WE CAN ALL GET ALONG IF ...

... we all eat at the same table together, not apart. We'll all get along better if we had a change of heart. And if we all do this, we'll get along better right from the very start!

— 14, Champaign, IL

... dieramos un poquito mas, sin esperar nada a cambio. (... everybody gave a little more without expecting to receive anything in return.)

— 24, Miami, FL

... we care about how others are feeling. We can take time to listen and really care about what we are hearing. Getting along means feeling other people's pain.

— 15, Decatur, IL

WE CAN ALL GET ALONG IF ...

... mutual respect prevails. We must all be considerate of individuality and seek the positive traits in each other.

— 17, Champaign, IL

... we stop projecting onto others our own opinions and values and accept others for who they are, not what we think they are.

— 16, Springfield, IL

... people let each other do their own thing.

— 14, Eugene, OR

WE CAN ALL GET ALONG IF ...

... restitution is paid, in one form or another, to the people who were enslaved for 400 years, robbed of respect, dignity and culture. We can all get along if one promise that has ever been made were kept (40 acres and a mule, jack). We can all get along if the oppressed were given the means to achieve, not just the useless, "You're free. Now go pursue the American Dream."

— Unknown

... the Sixties are revived.

— 16, Champaign, IL

WE CAN ALL GET ALONG IF ...

... everyone cares about feelings, and nobody cares about differences, when colors are defined but not made to stand out.

— 13, Edmonds, WA

... we communicate more and allow others to express themselves without attacking them.

— 33, Miami, FL

... if we got the chance to know each other.

— Urbana, IL

WE CAN ALL GET ALONG IF ...

... we got together and worked things out.

— 13, Boys Ranch, NM

... all the money in the world was distributed evenly.

— 14, Champaign, IL

... we are able to forgive one another.

— 88, Hialeah, FL

... people stop acting stupid and stop all the racism and violence and help this world be a better place for you and for me.

— 16, Urbana, IL

WE CAN ALL GET ALONG IF ...

... first we all admit that racism is still a problem—a problem that deserves our sincere attention. Racism affects everyone. Education for people of all ages is the key. We need to further educate adults, but especially we need to teach the children of our world. We need to teach equality for everyone.

— 12, Edmonds, WA

... people notice that bond that makes them all brothers and sisters.

— Unknown

... I moved far away.

— 15, Urbana, IL

WE CAN ALL GET ALONG IF ...

... mankind will follow the second greatest commandment of God—to love your neighbor as yourself.

— 27, Greenup, IL

... everyone could look at each other as just people instead of looking at their color or wondering what religion they were.

— 13, Eugene, OR

... we tolerate each other regardless of our differences.

— 16, Urbana, IL

WE CAN ALL GET ALONG IF ...

... we first understand ourselves and continually work to understand others.

— 21, St. Louis, MO

... people would just be themselves.

— 18, Bloomingdale, IL

... we would all realize that we all have the same feelings and we should help each other.

— 27, Miami, FL

WE CAN ALL GET ALONG IF ...

... you leave me alone.

— Unknown

... we all had a little bit of love.

— 15, Miami, FL

... we weren't so human.

— 13 1/2, Lynnwood, WA

... we end racism and try to work together to love one another.

— 17, Urbana, IL

WE CAN ALL GET ALONG IF ...

... normal mind functions once again prevail throughout the whole of our world.

— 62, Santa Fe, NM

... we realize that each of us is only a speck in the bigger picture of things rather than the center of the universe.

— 52, Bellair, IL

... people would just get it into their heads that no matter what race, culture or sex you are, people are people.

— 15, Urbana, IL

WE CAN ALL GET ALONG IF ...

... we cooperate and believe that we can work together without fighting or arguing and believe that God is there and always will be.

— 12, Urbana, IL

... we could learn the languages of all people.

— 10, Richmond, VA

... we all discard our prejudices and stop believing that our race deserves to be treated better than everybody else's.

— 14, Lynnwood, WA

WE CAN ALL GET ALONG IF ...

... everyone were more understanding and more accepting of other people and gave other people a chance, and not to live by how society expects us to be.

— 17, Urbana, IL

... we start trying to understand each other, to respect each other's costumes and ways of living, and learn to act correctly toward each other's feelings.

— 14, Curitiba, Brazil

... nobody would fight.

— 14, Champaign, IL

... we take care of our families
— 5, Richmond, V/

WE CAN ALL GET ALONG IF ...

... we get the time to know each other, care for each other and take time to listen.

— 37, Florida

... we respect others' ideas and opinions (even if we don't agree) and nurture everybody's talents so they can make a contribution to the world.

— Stanford, CA

... "please," "thank you" and "excuse me" were an active part of our vocabulary and if we would do *what* we say we will *when* we say we will.

— 52, Urbana, IL

WE CAN ALL GET ALONG IF ...

... we all stay out of other people's business.

— 17, Urbana, IL

... we choose to respect each person's right to live and believe differently than ourselves and we could understand that enjoyment of life doesn't come from others but from within ourselves.

— Columbus, OH

... everyone would stop killing each other and start loving each other.

— 11, Champaign, IL

WE CAN ALL GET ALONG IF ...

... we clean up our acts and attitudes. Let the kids act like kids, and let adults act like adults.

— 11, Urbana, IL

... we all accept differences. We should all come together like a melting pot and join each other's ideas, cultures and decisions.

— 19, Miami, FL

... people didn't start rumors and if people speak what they know instead of what they think they know.

— 14, Champaign, IL

WE CAN ALL GET ALONG IF ...

... we were all color-blind or if we saw with our hearts instead of our eyes.

— teenager, Arthur, IL

... everyone gets rid of their prejudice and selfish opinions and becomes more kind and compassionate.

— Unknown

... we would help each other.

— 12, Urbana, IL

WE CAN ALL GET ALONG IF ...

... I ruled the world. That is the only way different races can get along with each other.

— 14, Edmonds, WA

We never have gotten along, and I don't think we ever will.

— Urbana, IL

... people will look at others for what they are and not at the color of their skin or their race.

— 25, Miami, FL

WE CAN ALL GET ALONG IF ...

... every time you see somebody say hello and don't even worry about the color of their skin. Just say hello. It might not be much, but it is a start.

— Urbana, IL

... only we start to realize that God didn't pick and choose. He made us all together as one as brothers and sisters. We are all sinners, no matter who does what and how we do it. Treat every person right.

— 16, Jackson, MS

... people would stop thinking about themselves and think about other people first.

— 12, Champaign, IL

WE CAN ALL GET ALONG IF ...

... people of different relations would look at one another and see themselves.

— 17, Urbana, IL

... we let the children lead the way.

— 34, Hickory Hills, IL

... before we recognize difference, we recognize sameness and the fact that on the same fundamental level, before we are anything else, we are all Homo sapiens; and if we realize our inevitable reliance on each other.

— 20, Madison, WI

WE CAN ALL GET ALONG IF ...

... we look to see the real person inside of others—the person underneath.

— 49, Urbana, IL

... for once, people would look through one's differences and at our similarities.

— 19, Morristown, NY

... the world was perfect. But it is not and we are human, so the world will never get along.

— 14, Champaign, IL

WE CAN ALL GET ALONG IF ...

... we give positive value to life and help others as much as we help ourselves.

— 62, Santa Fe, NM

... we learn to communicate with each other. Racism and other discriminations are born from fear and lack of understanding. If we all explained our feelings and points of view, everyone would start to understand and become more tolerant of the people around us.

— 14, Edmonds, WA

... we respect each other and follow God's way.

— 18, Urbana, IL

WE CAN ALL GET ALONG IF ...

... we would learn to understand and accept each other as we are and not try to change each other like we do.

— 24, Miami, FL

... we realize that the way to succeed is not to step on other people to get to the top.

— teenager, Arthur, IL

... we all work together and never give up.

— Urbana, IL

WE CAN ALL GET ALONG IF ...

... we have more things that have black people involved in, have people try to say hi and treat them as they would like to be treated.

— Unknown

... everyone wants to help and succeeds just a little bit.

— 17, Urbana, IL

... we follow the Golden Rule: Do unto others as you would have them do unto you.

— Honolulu, HI

WE CAN ALL GET ALONG IF ...

... we show each other respect and courtesy and try to understand each other's beliefs.

— 17, Urbana, IL

... we play together nicely.

— 11

... we want to. (I realize this is simplistic, but as I compose this long sentence about stopping the laying of blame, the stereotyping, etc., all I could hear was my son's voice when he was 2 saying, "We can if we want to." Somehow, I think that says it all.)

— Los Angeles, CA

WE CAN ALL GET ALONG IF ...

... each individual human being will think about what inalienable rights humans possess and then work in their own lives to see that they never transgress against someone else's rights and that the society in which we live does not.

— Unknown

... the people of this country would just calm down.

— 10, Urbana, IL

... we don't expect more than we have worked for.

— 40, Port Orford, OR

WE CAN ALL GET ALONG IF ...

... everyone will begin to understand that it is not what people look like on the outside but their redeeming qualities on the inside.

— 14, Urbana, IL

... we count to 10 when angry, to 100 when really angry and try to spend some time every day with someone we don't know very well, just listening and asking questions.

— 31, Troy, NY

... we hire police officers and firefighters to serve in the neighborhoods in which they live.

— 34, Hickory Hills, IL

We Can All Get Along If ...

... we all wake up and realize that we're all the same underneath the skin.

— 15, Champaign, IL

... everyone was treated equal no matter what their color, even if they were purple with green hair.

— 15, Indianapolis, IN

... everyone knew what the other one was going through. Many of the racial problems are not just in America but all across the world and are mostly caused by misunderstanding people.

— 14, Edmonds, WA

WE CAN ALL GET ALONG IF ...

... everyone would see that it's good to be different.

— 11, Urbana, IL

... we accept others for their different points of view and love them for being different.

— Hill Air Force Base, UT

... people could be friends instead of enemies.

— 11, Tolono, IL

... we all realize that we are the same inside.

— 13, Champaign, IL

WE CAN ALL GET ALONG IF ...

... people stop trying to place the blame for their problems on others and instead face up to them and if people listen to what the other is saying instead of just yelling and screaming at each other.

— 18, Minot, ND

... we could be a little less stuck on ourselves and see that a variety of people makes the world less bland.

— Unknown

... we learn that we can't always get what we want.

— 13, Urbana, IL

... we hold hands with each other.
— 6, Richmond, VA

WE CAN ALL GET ALONG IF ...

... we lived by natural law. We wouldn't need the help of technology. We would only hunt for our food, go back to our caves and sleep peacefully. Eliminate technology and we wouldn't be so greedy about material possessions.

— 17, Hialeah, FL

... the alternative to violence was taught by parents to their children while they are still young.

— 16, Urbana, IL

WE CAN ALL GET ALONG IF ...

... we would all be kind to each other, mind our own business and keep our comments to ourselves.

— teenager, Indianapolis, IN

... everyone were treated fairly.

— 11, Urbana, IL

... the Caucasians and Latinos would unite as one; that way we could progress together.

— 13, Los Angeles, CA

WE CAN ALL GET ALONG IF ...

... we all learned to be more tolerant and tried to understand each other.

— Unknown

... we don't get mad at people for their color because we're all the same inside.

— 10, Urbana, IL

... we would try to develop an understanding of the differences that we all possess as individuals.

— 35, Eagan, MN

WE CAN ALL GET ALONG IF ...

... we can share a common belief and goal and work together harmoniously.

— 17, Belleville, IL

... we do what we say we will; we are on time; we make clover chains together; we are honest; and we genetically breed out dogs' ability to bark.

— 17, Urbana, IL

... we learned not to gossip and spread rumors about people.

— teenager, Indianapolis, IN

WE CAN ALL GET ALONG IF ...

... we all try and do our part and clean up our areas a little bit.

— 10, Urbana, IL

... we recognize the danger of greed and anger and if we realize the true joy of being happy rather than being mad.

— Unknown

... we all cared about each other.

— 13, Champaign, IL

WE CAN ALL GET ALONG IF ...

... we stop depersonalizing others. You cannot fully hate and want to torture someone else if you believe his or her humanity to be equal to your own.

— 39, Austin, TX

... we don't fight over dumb things.

— 14, Champaign, IL

... there would be more laws and if someone did something wrong, they would go to jail. More people should start to respect each others' rights.

— 11, Urbana, IL

WE CAN ALL GET ALONG IF ...

... we treat everyone respectfully and bond together with a common vision of equality while standing up for the American way: Freedom—let it reign!

— 20, Tampa, FL

... all people could respect each others' property.

— 15, Champaign, IL

... punishments are increased for hate crimes and kids are made aware that hate crimes are bad (but not through school).

— 14, Eugene, OR

WE CAN ALL GET ALONG IF ...

... all gangs will join together in one gang that will help everyone.

— 17, Los Angeles, CA

... everyone could be nice to one another. Also, we could get along by stopping all the violence. Another way we could get along is if no one was prejudiced on skin color. We can also get along if everyone got rid of drugs and alcohol.

— 14, Brady, TX

... we can pass up our differences and pinpoint our likenesses.

— 16, Urbana, IL

WE CAN ALL GET ALONG IF ...

... we first put other people before ourselves. One should give of oneself, not just of his pocket.

— Unknown

... we learn to put our own needs aside for a season, look into the eyes and right down to the soul of others and see how the Spirit of this universe has blessed them. There, we'll discover how much we are alike, particularly the longing for human companionship and play. Anger is defeated by play.

— 46, Urbana, IL

WE CAN ALL GET ALONG IF ...

... we all considered people's feelings and accepted them for who they are, not their color, race or religion. People tend to stereotype people and put them in a box and that's where they stay.

— 14, San Gabriel, CA

... we will stop recognizing color or creed and start recognizing the person for themselves. We can learn a lot from people if we get by the way they look.

— 35, Lawrenceville, IL

WE CAN ALL GET ALONG IF ...

... everyone would understand everybody else. People wouldn't go around commenting on other people by putting them down or hurting their feelings.

— 14, Champaign, IL

... people would stop trying to rule other people. Everybody should think about other people's feelings and opinions and try to be fair and not judge without knowing the situation.

— 13, Compton, CA

... we have love, unity, respect and no prejudice or racism in our hearts.

— 17, Urbana, IL

WE CAN ALL GET ALONG IF ...

... we could work together to make the world a better place.

— 14, Champaign, IL

... we stopped thinking one race is better than the next and governments stopped taking advantage of their power.

— teenager, Indianapolis, IN

... we understand where each of our points of view are coming from.

— 15, Millstadt, IL

... people stop using drugs.

— 10, Urbana, IL

WE CAN ALL GET ALONG IF ...

... people would just accept people as human beings instead of having racism and prejudice.

— 14, Champaign, IL

... we would first stop to think how it would be to be in the other person's shoes and then respond with words or actions.

— 28, Tualatin, OR

... we keep our noses out of other people's business and if we play with everyone and not leave anyone out.

— 10, Urbana, IL

WE CAN ALL GET ALONG IF ...

... everyone left everyone else well enough alone and in peace. Be excellent to each other. Party on, dude!

— 22, Rohnert Park, CA

... we would not be mean to people.

— Unknown

... we learn to look over other people's differences and faults and judge people for who they really are.

— 17, Urbana, IL

WE CAN ALL GET ALONG IF ...

... people would be nice and not be so pushy and bossy.

— 14, Champaign, IL

... we use the Bible as our standard of living and follow Jesus' example.

— 25, Savoy, IL

... we love our neighbors as ourselves and if people were more willing to sacrifice.

— 17, Urbana, IL

... everyone could see the beauty of uniqueness.

— 16, Minot, ND

WE CAN ALL GET ALONG IF ...

... we are willing to treat the other person as we would like to be treated, which is one of the guidelines given by our Heavenly Father to guide us to the best life if we would just obey. Instead, we think we know a better way. Why do we most always think we "know it all"? We attribute that thought many times to our teenagers, but they get it pretty honest.

— 83, Robinson, IL

... respeto mutuo entre las personas, comprendiendo los caracteres de cada cual y no entrometerse en la vida privada de nadie. (... we have mutual respect for people and understand the character of others and not get involved in other people's private life.)

— 45, Miami, FL

WE CAN ALL GET ALONG IF ...

... we all drank the same kind of Gatorade.

— 13, Lynnwood, WA

... people would stop being so pig-headed and open their ears and minds.

— 18, Urbana, IL

... we take the time to listen to each other and act based on what we jointly understand to be true.

— Livingston, NJ

... the world was cleaner.

— 13, Champaign, IL

... we shar
together
— 5
Richmond
V

WE CAN ALL GET ALONG IF ...

... you don't accept people for what you think you can mold them into, keep an open mind and understand that everyone is different.

— 16, Urbana, IL

... somebody would assure that nobody is left out by anybody because nobody deserves the disrespect of anybody and somebody has to assure it.

— 35, Cumberland, MD

... we try to agree with each other.

— 15, Champaign, IL

WE CAN ALL GET ALONG IF ...

It all depends on whether we want to get along. If we were to get along, it would be a miracle. People who are different from each other sometimes expect too much from each other.

— Unknown

... people believed that there could be world peace.

— 17, Urbana, IL

... only our parents taught us how!

— 57, Albany, NY

... people would at least try to get along.

— 14, Champaign, IL

WE CAN ALL GET ALONG IF ...

... we could learn to tolerate, as well as appreciate, the differences in others. We should attempt to treat people as individuals instead of trying to stereotype them as members of certain racial, ethnic or religious groups. Differences make life interesting, if not intriguing.

— 25, Cleveland, OH

... everyone could be heard and if we would listen better.

— 17, Urbana, IL

... there wasn't any violence, people were friendly, there were no putdowns, there were no guns, there were no bad gangs and everybody played sports.

— teenager, Indianapolis, IN

WE CAN ALL GET ALONG IF ...

... everyone could learn to tolerate the imperfections of life instead of being angered by them.

— 17, Urbana, IL

... we think about others and their feelings instead of being selfish and ignorant.

— 16, Champaign, IL

... ignorant people quit banning together to protect their ignorant ways and promoting such.

— 62, Santa Fe, NM

WE CAN ALL GET ALONG IF ...

... we respect another's differences (whether they be racial, religious, cultural or moral differences), accept people for themselves and don't infringe on their individuality.

— 18, Urbana, IL

...we can respect others' ideas and opinions and customs without prejudice.

— 16, Champaign, IL

... the bloody Americans stopped thinking they were the only people in the world with Internet access.

— 23, Sydney, Australia

WE CAN ALL GET ALONG IF ...

... we forgive and forget.

— 16, Urbana, IL

... we practice the Golden Rule: Do unto others as you would have them do unto you.

— 65, West York, IL

I don't know how we could all get along.

— teenager, Indianapolis, IN

WE CAN ALL GET ALONG IF ...

... people would stop thinking of themselves and pull together with a single, united cause. This would take dedication, cooperation and willingness to put down the weapons of destruction and pick up the tools to rebuild the America that we were once famous for.

— 16, Urbana, IL

... we learn to accept the United States as a salad bowl, not a melting pot. We can never change people's histories. We should learn to accept everyone as having a separate heritage like lettuce, carrots and tomatoes in a salad that never become one.

— 15, Millstadt, IL

WE CAN ALL GET ALONG IF ...

... we were brought up better by our parents.

— teenager, Indianapolis, IN

... we don't pick on kids that aren't your age. Don't be rude.

— 11, Urbana, IL

... amandonos como familia como Dios no ama. (... we love each other as family like God loves us.)

— 51, Miami, FL

... everyone realizes that God made all of us the same.

— 16

WE CAN ALL GET ALONG IF ...

... everyone stopped judging other people and started trying to make things better than they are.

— teenager, Indianapolis, IN

... people realized how boring the world would be if everyone was the same.

— 18, Urbana, IL

... people could share things instead of fighting over them.

— 15, Champaign, IL

... everyone stops being violent and lends a hand in things.

— teenager, Arthur, IL

WE CAN ALL GET ALONG IF ...

... we need not be equal in number, but equal in mind and spirit.

— 18, Urbana, IL

... people would try to drop all the hatred and revenge and just try to be nice to each other for once.

— 16, Champaign, IL

... we can look deeper than the outer covering and into the true hearts and minds of those around us.

— teenager, Arthur, IL

... we started taking better care of the things we have.

— teenager, Indianapolis, IN

WE CAN ALL GET ALONG IF ...

... we put God first and realize that we first have to learn to get along with ourselves. If we can get along with ourselves first, there's no need to try with anyone else.

— 34, Tickfaw, LA

... we put all differences aside and partied.

— 14, Eugene, OR

... there is the desire by everyone to get along. If people acted in a civil manner, others wouldn't have to suffer for their actions.

— 17, Urbana, IL

WE CAN ALL GET ALONG IF ...

... we try to remember that the ultimate struggle is that of mankind and the universe, not man against man. Whether the relationship with the universe is with us or against us is up to us as humans to determine.

— 30, Indianapolis, IN

... we be friends. We know each other better.

— 11, Urbana, IL

... being different becomes interesting rather than fear-provoking, disagreement is not taken as a mark of disaffection, and we quit covering our insecurity with rejecting bravado.

— 54, Chicago, IL

WE CAN ALL GET ALONG IF ...

... we would stop being so stubborn and stop thinking just of ourselves.

— 17, Urbana, IL

... everyone would only accept others as they are and try to help one another.

— teenager, Arthur, IL

... people would give up trying to change other people's cultures into more acceptable, "mainstream" extensions of their culture and just resign themselves to the fact that everybody is different and that there's nothing wrong with that.

— 16, Champaign, IL

WE CAN ALL GET ALONG IF ...

... we learn to accept, or at least respect, each other. Respect and acceptance are the basis for trust and harmony, which this world needs badly.

— 14, Edmonds, WA

... everybody would quit being stuck on stupid.

— 18, Urbana, IL

... everybody keeps out of my way. (Not what you had in mind, I suppose.) Pop psychology No. 725: I blame the parents.

— 38, Manchester, England

WE CAN ALL GET ALONG IF ...

... we stopped arguing.

— 17, Champaign, IL

... people did not act so silly and if we all stuck together and if people minded their own business.

— East St. Louis, IL

... we go fishing.

— 11, Urbana, IL

... we look for some way to help someone else each day.

— 39

WE CAN ALL GET ALONG IF ...

... we help each other and show that we care and don't quarrel with each other.

— 16, Champaign, IL

... we plant seeds of kindness and caring when dealing with others of all faiths. Praise each other, and especially praise your children so that they feel good about themselves. Most of all, try your very best each day to be a better person and remember that a cup of kindness always eases another person's sorrow.

— Vandalia, IL

... we search for the beauty inside rather than the wealth on the outside.

— 17, Urbana, IL

WE CAN ALL GET ALONG IF ...

... people could take their anger out on something else than on another human.

— 10, Urbana, IL

... people open up to each other.

— Unknown

... we don't judge people.

— 15, Champaign, IL

... we imagine possibilities for change.

— 35, Santa Fe, NM

... we play together.
— 5, Richmond, VA

... we quit blaming "Murphy Brown."

— 34, Hickory Hills, IL

... understanding and compromise were the first priorities.

— 16, Champaign, IL

... we learn unconditional love. There's no way we can have peace in the world until people learn to accept others for who they are, not what they should have been, because that's how God made people, and who are you to argue with God?

— 13, Lynnwood, WA

WE CAN ALL GET ALONG IF ...

...we learn to accept everyone for who they are and not what they are. We must also get rid of all the stereotypes that we have about people in general.

— 18, Urbana, IL

... we put ourselves in the other person's shoes for a while.

— Rochester, NY

... we stop separating ourselves into groups and all live together as a society.

— 15, Champaign, IL

WE CAN ALL GET ALONG IF ...

... everybody was like I am supposed to be.

— 18, Maasbree, the Netherlands

... we'd all realize that while you're in someone else's backyard looking at their leaves, you need to be in your own backyard raking your own.

— 17, Urbana, IL

... everybody could drink guarana (a Brazilian soft drink) every day.

— 17, Sao Paulo, Brazil

... everyone belonged to the same country club.

— 18, Urbana, IL

WE CAN ALL GET ALONG IF ...

... love fills the air

And we're treated like equals, fair and square

In a place where respect reigns

And dignity is gained

Where we have no wars

Or crack stores

No AIDS

Hand grenades

No colors

Just shades.

— 17, Urbana, IL

124

U*nder the guidance of their teacher,* Ray Elliott, *the following students and recent graduates of Urbana High School in Urbana, Illinois, contributed to the making of this book for the Tales cultural journalism project:*

Jonathan Bach; Ben Burrus; Angela Deaville; Courtney Fifer; Matt Foster; Sara Foster; Dagmar Heftrig; Adriana Hernandez; Sarah Livingston; Erica Morrow; Mary Christine Newman; Craig Peache; Anne Peterson; Mike Reuter; Christina Rotramel; Rob Scharlau; Alex Trujillo; Debbie Uchtmann; Matt Vyverberg; Karen Webber; Nikkol Welch; Amanda Wiziecki; Linda Wolfe; and Jenny Wolfersberger.

Thanks to all of the people who offered their responses for consideration, and to teacher Barbara F. Wood and her students at Bensley Elementary School in Richmond, Virginia, for the drawings that appear in this book.

Do you have a response to "We can all get along if ..."? Send it, along with your name, age, town, state and country (if other than the United States), to the following address:

> *Project Get Along*
> *c/o Tales, inc.*
> *R.R. 2, Box 401*
> *Urbana, IL 61801*

Responses may be used in a future, revised edition of this book.